ANIMAL CHILDREN

edited by
Roger Caras
foreword by
Roger Tory Peterson

S.Jacobsen

Westover
Publishing Company

An affiliate of Media General, Richmond, Va.

Cover: Photograph of
a Mother Llama
and her young.
Photo by Toni Angermayer

Prepared in cooperation with
Photo Researchers, Inc.,
New York, New York.

Book design by Sylvan Jacobson

INTRODUCTION

Men are really extraordinary animals. While we have on the one hand been acting with incredible indifference and even outright cruelty toward the animal kingdom, we have never lost our love for the individual animals that constitute its masses. We have exterminated species upon species, yet we are moved to affection when we see a baby animal. People who will sanction a steer being hung from the beams by one hind leg while its throat is slit in a slaughterhouse will urge their children to feed a baby cow a bottle of milk in a local children's zoo. I once saw a woman standing in front of a cage wearing a leopard skin coat enthralled by a leopard nursing her cubs. It really was quite extraordinary.

What are we, then, unfeeling, or are we hypocrites who feel yet deny emotion? Do we perhaps see something quite different when we look at a baby—something different from the adult form? One thing seems clear enough. Unless we adopt a more uniform attitude toward the survival of all animals—young or grown—there won't be a baby anything around fifty years from now.

This book is a tribute to whatever it is in us that "turns on" at the sight of baby animals. Perhaps what we are saluting here—and hoping to satisfy —is a lingering shred of a former humanity. Or, better yet, perhaps it is the harbinger of things to come on the human emotional horizon. Just think what the world could be like if we felt toward all living creatures what we feel for their young—toward all men what we feel for human children. Not only animals, but even we might survive ourselves!

Roger Caras

FOREWORD

Most young things are appealing, eliciting in us feelings of tenderness and affection. But newborn birds and mammals fall into two rather distinct categories: those that are naked, blind and rather repulsive, such as mice, squirrels, sparrows, and pelicans; and those that are fluffy, bright-eyed and cuddly right from the start, such as young hares, fawns and baby ducks.

Those born naked and blind have a relatively short period of development before birth and a longer period of dependence on the parent afterward. On the other hand, those that are born with fur or down and can fend for themselves rather quickly, have a longer period of pre-natal development.

One of the things that makes young animals so engaging is their love of play. But what is the significance of play? A kitten pouncing on a ball (as it would a mouse), a young sea lion sparring with another youngster its age, or young deer engaging in chasing games—all seem to point to a sort of juvenile training along lines that will be useful to survival later on.

Some young animals reach maturity much more slowly than others. Whereas a young Japanese coturnix quail may itself have a brood when only a few weeks old, a royal albatross will not mate and lay its first egg until its eighth or ninth year. A female meadow vole may reproduce when it is only a month old, but an Indian elephant must wait at least 15 years.

The highest mortality is during the early weeks and months of life. Being young is not easy, but it has its moments of fun.

Roger Tory Peterson
Old Lyme, Connecticut

Vicuna

"Just as young mammals depend upon their mothers for nourishment and education so do they for their psychological development. Animals reared artificially away from their mothers are slower at learning and less active than their normal siblings; social or gregarious animals brought up in isolation without the companionship of other young animals and their parents are so deformed in their behaviour patterns that they cannot rejoin their species when mature—they are so deranged that in human terms they are mentally unbalanced."

From *The Life of Mammals* by L. Harrison Matthews, Vol. 1 (Weidenfeld and Nicholson, London, 1969).

Black Rhinoceros

"The females are particularly patient with their single offspring which accompanies them for two years or perhaps more, long after the parental milk supply has ceased. I have watched these young animals, with a sizeable horn on their nose, butting away into their mother's inguinal region in a vain attempt to obtain some milk. The long-suffering parents made no attempt to drive them away, unlike many animals that seem to us to display an unnecessarily harsh attitude towards their suckling young. The calves make a mewing noise which sounds rather plaintive; it is seldom heard in the adult animals which usually only snort and grunt."

From *Animals of East Africa* by C. A. Spinage (Collins, London, 1962).

Wild Turkey

"It is interesting to note his movements when he discovers that he is alone; that his 'mammy' and his mates are gone. He raises himself up, looks with his keen eyes in every direction for the flock, and, failing to discover them, gives the well-known coarse cluck. Then he raises his head high in the air, and listens intently for his mother's call."

From "Hunting the Wild Turkey" by "Clip" (*American Field,* 1886, 26:409–410, 433–434).

Barn Owls

"The fuzzy white nestling down is the only covering of the young barn owl until about the sixth day. At this time the buff-colored second downy plumage begins to appear, and carries the earlier down away on its tips. This second down rapidly develops into the thick, woolly covering which is so characteristic of young barn owls, and remains as a conspicuous feature until the bird is about fifty days of age."

From "The Growth of Some Young Raptorial Birds" by Eustace Lowell Sumner Jr. (*Univ. Calif. Publ. Zool.,* 1933, Vol. 40).

Screech Owls

"Once outside the nest, the problems are not over for
either owlets or their parents. Survival is not just a matter
of flying, because the fledglings must first of all learn how
to hunt efficiently and this takes time. In tawny owls at
least, the parents must supply their offspring with voles
and mice well into autumn, and it is not until then that
the juveniles make their own way in the world. Months
of trial and error will have made some of them reasonably
skillful in the art of being killers. . . ."

From *Owls: Their Natural and Unnatural History* by
John Sparks and Tony Soper (Taplinger Publishing,
New York, 1970).

Sea Lion

"On land the bulls paid very little attention to the pups, but when the pups entered the water the bulls showed a strong protective instinct. If a pup started to swim out into deep water, a bull headed it off and chased it back landwards. . . . In some of the localities where sea lions are observed, notably on Cedros Island, frightened pups would rush for their fathers, and start nuzzling up to them. The bulls returned the nuzzling, and appeared concerned for the welfare of the youngsters. . . ."

From *Seals of the World* by Gavin Maxwell (Houghton Mifflin, Boston, 1967).

Porpoise

"Naturally, whales also render assistance to the young, and not only their own. In marineland, when a new-born calf is slow in swimming to the surface, it is pushed up either by its mother or by another cow. The same behavior was also displayed towards a still-born calf, and is said to be quite common among Bottlenose Dolphins in their natural state. Moore reported a number of instances of Bottlenoses continuing to push a dead calf or at least its head to the surface for days after it was dead."

From *Whales* by E. J. Slijper (Basic Books, New York, 1962).

13

Ass

One of the things that may make us feel closer to the mammals—besides the fact that we are mammals ourselves—is that their means for expression are so similar to our own. We can understand the way a young ass acts toward his mother—and we approve of it—but what of, say, a turtle? We must admit it is something of an enigma to us. We can accept academically that a turtle doesn't love his mother—but how do we handle the fact emotionally?

Sea Turtle

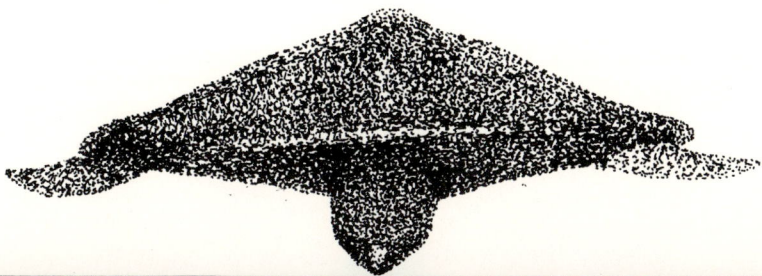

Kangaroo

"The young approaches from the mother's front and begins feeling for the pouch. . . . When it finds the pouch rim it grasps it and goes in head first, turns a complete somersault, and brings the head toward the entrance. If the young is temporarily lost, the mother runs around looking for it and calls loudly. The young also calls loudly and this call brings not only its mother but other female kangaroos up to it. When the young is found, the mother adopts the posture which facilitates entry to the pouch and at the same time produces a special clucking call."

From *Kangaroos* by H. J. Frith and J. H. Calaby (Humanities Press, New York, 1969).

Alligator

"All crocodilians hatch out from eggs, which in the wild are buried by the females in shallow pits on the shores of lakes and rivers or in heaps of decaying vegetation. There are usually between twenty and a hundred white eggs which, according to species, are about the size of a hen or a goose egg. The shell is solid and very porous. . . . Before hatching, the young have a sharp horny outgrowth, the egg-tooth, on the front part of the muzzle, with which they cut through the hard eggshell. The eggtooth falls off soon after they have left the egg."

From *Reptiles and Amphibians* by Zdenek Vogel (The Viking Press, New York, 1964).

Baboons

"During its first week, the baby is closely protected by its mother, who may turn her back or walk away from other curious members of the troop. . . . Her attention to her newborn is constant. She picks through its hair continually with infinite patience, licks it, and indulges in a great amount of lip-smacking, thought to be a gesture of pacification. . . . observers have seen babies sit erect by the end of their second week, and after three weeks run about on wobbly legs, although occasionally six weeks may pass before the child touches the ground."

From *Almost Human* by Julie Macdonald (Chilton Books, Philadelphia, 1965).

Black Racer

One thing we must never do, of course, is assign human emotions to animals. They are *not* like us, but what are they like? I can accept the fact that a mother snake doesn't feel about her offspring the way a woman feels about her children. But what, if anything, does the snake feel? Or can it be true that the snake "feels" nothing at all? Perhaps the very idea of feeling is far too human for so low a beast. Or, could it be that just because we cannot look into a snake's eyes the way we look into a dog's and see something we can comprehend, we say automatically—"no feeling"?

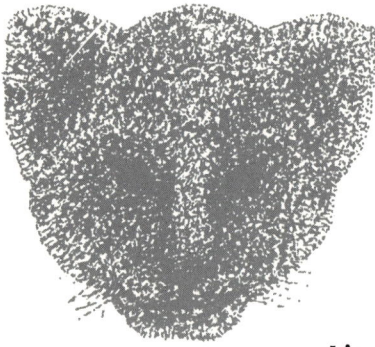

Lions

"When I had recovered from the shock he took me to Elsa's grave. It was under a tree close to the tents, overlooking the river and the sand-bank where Elsa had introduced me to her children. This was the tree on whose rough bark the cubs had learned to sharpen their claws; under the shade of which the family had so often played...."

From *Forever Free* by Joy Adamson (Harcourt Brace Jovanovich, New York, 1962).

Flying Squirrel

"The baby squirrels climbed about in the nest now. One day two of them ventured out of the nest hole and onto the bark-covered trunk of the fir tree. One youngster tumbled unhurt to the forest floor. The other baby managed to cling to the bark until rescued by its mother. Quick to respond to her babies' squeaks of distress, the mother flying squirrel first plucked the baby off the bark, then glided down to the forest floor and with her nose and forepaws rolled her baby into a ball. Picking it up by the lateral skinfold of its gliding skinfold, she scurried back up to the nest and poked her offspring through the hole."

From *Squirrels of North America* by Dorcas MacClintock (Van Nostrand Reinhold Co., New York, 1970).

Armadillo

"Strangely, the armadillo bears identical quadruplets, all
of one sex. If the mother has 'twins' she bears eight
identical babies, again all of one sex. . . . The young are
born with their eyes open, and within a day or two are
tottering after their mother. They continue to nurse for
two months, well after they have started eating insects. . . .
At birth the armadillo's skin is soft and flexible and shows
the pattern its shell will eventually have. As the animal
matures, its armor hardens."

From *North American Mammals* by Roger A. Caras
(Meredith Press, New York, 1967).

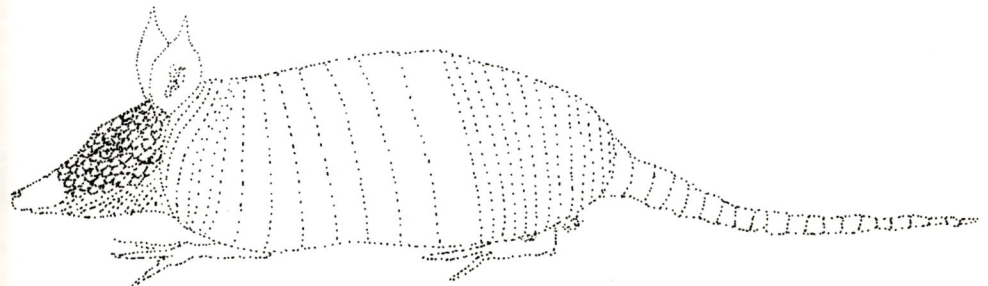

Hawaiian Monk Seal

"Pups are produced throughout the first six months of the year, but chiefly between the middle of March and the end of May. They are about 36 pounds in weight and 3 ft. 2 ins. in length at birth. The coat is of soft black hair which is moulted at approximately three to five weeks to one that is silvery blue grey dorsally, shading to silvery white ventrally. Suckling continues for about five weeks, at the end of which time the pup weighs 139 pounds. It is then deserted by its mother, who is believed to fast during the nursing period, and left to fend for itself."

From *Seals of the World* by Judith E. King (The British Museum [Natural History], London, 1964).

Raccoon

"Little raccoons spend a great deal of their time sleeping, usually in a big pile, sharing each other's body heat. When one of the top layer of babies becomes cold, it just shifts around until it has gotten to the bottom of the heap. The weight of its brothers and sisters is not heavy enough to cause it any inconvenience."

From *The World of the Raccoon* by Leonard Lee Rue III (J. P. Lippincott, Philadelphia, 1964).

Polar Bears

"These initial all-important days are mainly devoted to
accustoming the cubs to their new environment and
strengthening them by various forms of play—in addition
to digging down into the snow for grass—the elevation at
the outer end of the den's entrance-passage serving as a
practice climbing-pitch and tobogganing slide. Later, the
cubs' play can be extended to sliding down the nearest
ice-slope on their bellies with legs outstretched fore and
aft, in imitation perhaps of their mother sliding with them.
This is repeated again and again."

From *The World of the Polar Bear* by Richard
Perry (Cassell, London, 1966).

Dormouse   Pygmy Hippo

From the instant of birth, the baby animal must undertake
an astonishing assignment. Of all the millions of ways of
life that have evolved on earth, only one is exactly right
for each infant and its task is to learn that unique way of
life so well that survival is assured—at least long enough to
produce another generation of babies to be given the
same assignment. Survival must seem like an overwhelming
job for most babies, with so many forces combined
against them.

Frigate Bird

"Frigate-Birds or 'Man-O-War Hawks' are the pirates and scavengers of the tropical islands. . . . During the breeding season they will 'work' colonies of nesting terns, flapping slowly over the nesting areas and snatching up chicks without pausing to settle, disposing of a youngster in two or three large gulps. Not infrequently they will find on return to their own nest that a neighbourly Frigate has seized the opportunity to gobble up their own egg."

From *Seabirds in Southern Waters* by HRH The Prince Philip, Duke of Edinburgh (Harper & Row, New York, 1962).

White Stork

"The gaping of young is one of the stimuli that creates an
ardent desire to feed them in the adults of many species.
The young, in turn, are stimulated at a very early age to
gape, by such signals as vibration of the nest and later by
the sight and shape of the parent's head. Like other parts
of birds which serve as sign stimuli, the mouths of nestlings
are brightly colored and have great contrast."

From *Bird* by Lois and Louis Darling (Houghton
Mifflin, Boston, 1962).

Llama

"The other members of the camel family live in western and southern South America, usually at high altitudes. The Guanaco and the Vicuna are the only ones that are still wild—the Llama and the Alpaca are domesticated. . . . Both the Llama and the Guanaco are common in zoos and both breed readily in captivity; indeed, a big-eyed, gentle, imperious baby Llama is one of the most charming of animal babies. The Alpaca and the dainty Vicuna are less common."

From *The Bronx Zoo Book of Wild Animals* by William Bridges (Golden Press, New York, 1968).

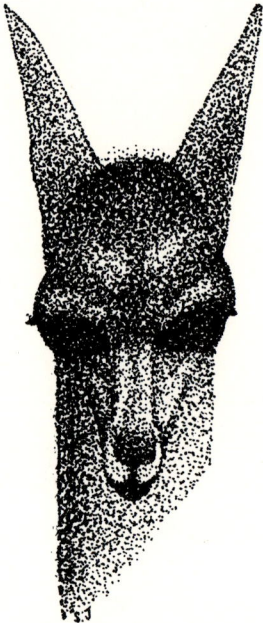

Yellow-Haired Porcupine

One of the strangest and perhaps most ironic aspects of our attitude toward animals is our way of looking at their young. We may hate some animals as adults, but seldom as babies. This seems to be particularly true with mammals and birds—perhaps because they are warm-blooded, like us. But even animals that we will never look upon as beautiful or appealing are somehow "cute" when they are young. Maybe we see qualities of the young of our own species when we look upon, say, a porcupine.

Gibraltar Apes

The tie between parents and their young is so incredibly strong in some animals it is hard to conceive that it is totally lacking in others. A monkey is no more successful an animal, really, than a rattlesnake or a salmon, yet the latter two creatures have the maternal instincts of anthracite. The monkey, on the other hand, would not, could not survive physically or emotionally without what we must call mother-love.

Ostrich

The children of birds generally look less like their parents, it seems, than the children of mammals. That is because young mammals usually do not shed their "coats" dramatically and assume adult covering the way birds do. It is not very difficult to know you are looking at a baby elephant or a baby bear, but when faced with a parcel of chicks one can often do little more than scratch one's head and wait to see what the next molt will bring.

Koala

"Like all marsupials, the newly born koala is extremely small, measuring barely ¾ inch and weighing about 5½ grammes, with the fore-limbs more developed than the hind-limbs to help it cling to the mother's fur on its instinctive journey upwards into the pouch. On leaving the teat at about six months the animal is well furred and about 7 inches long; it continues in the pouch for another two months, afterwards clinging to its mother's back and being hugged closely to her when resting, until about a year old."

From "The Koala" by Ellis Troughton, in *A Treasury of Australian Wildlife* edited by D. F. McMichael (Ure Smith, Sydney, 1968).

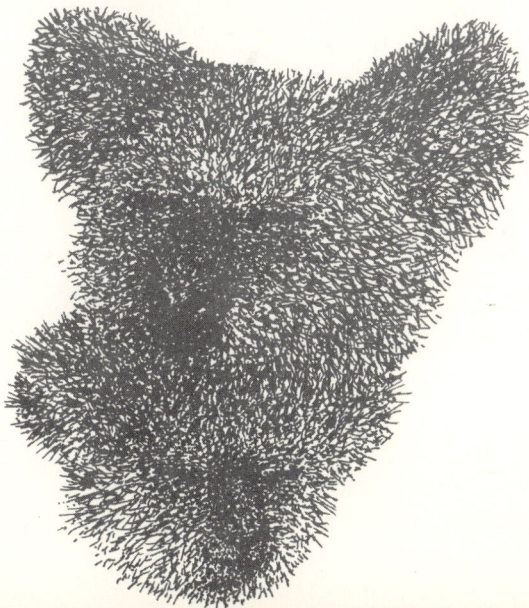

Baboons

It is very difficult when watching animal mothers with their young not to see in them a reflection of ourselves—or, perhaps, see in ourselves a reflection of them. At no time is it more difficult to avoid the cardinal error of anthropomorphism than when watching the often tender relationship between animal mother and animal child.

Cheetah

"At the age of three weeks I first heard the cubs
make a high-pitched chirp. . . . They were calling
Pippa who appeared after ten minutes; the cubs
then tumbled all over her and stood on their
hind legs, embracing and licking her head.
One was especially affectionate and finally
cuddled cosily beneath her shin, engulfed
between her chest and front legs. It defended
its position and in a comic way by spitting at the
other cubs whenever they came close."

From *The Spotted Sphinx* by Joy
Adamson (Collins & Harvill Press,
London, 1969).

Giraffe

"After the birth the mother is normally very solicitous and immediately starts to clean her baby. A healthy calf is able to stand within five minutes and begins to feed twenty minutes later. . . . For the first ten days the baby suckles at fairly long intervals and the milk is accordingly right and concentrated, later it suckles on demand when the milk changes to a third of its original fat content and half the protein. . . . Suckling continues for nine to ten months although the calf starts sampling solid food after three weeks, having already nibbled at things within a few days of birth. . . ."

From *The Book of the Giraffe* by C. A. Spinage (Houghton Mifflin, Boston, 1968).

Willow Warblers

"Young birds grow to adult size remarkably quickly compared with reptiles or mammals—in as little as two weeks in the case of some of the smaller, open-nesting song-birds. . . . But it is difficult to say when they are fully grown, for there is seldom any clear indication. Even when a bird has reached adult body weight, it is often not fully developed in other ways. . . . "

From *Book of British Birds* (Drive Publications Ltd., London, 1969).

Old Squaw

"When searching for food, they [old squaw ducks] string out in a long line and swim abreast. At a signal one at the extreme end goes down, the rest follow in regular time, never all at once, and rarely more than two or three at a time. The last one goes down in his turn with the regularity of clockwork. . . ."

> From *The Ducks, Geese and Swans of North America* by Francis H. Kortright (Stackpole Company, Harrisburg, 1942).

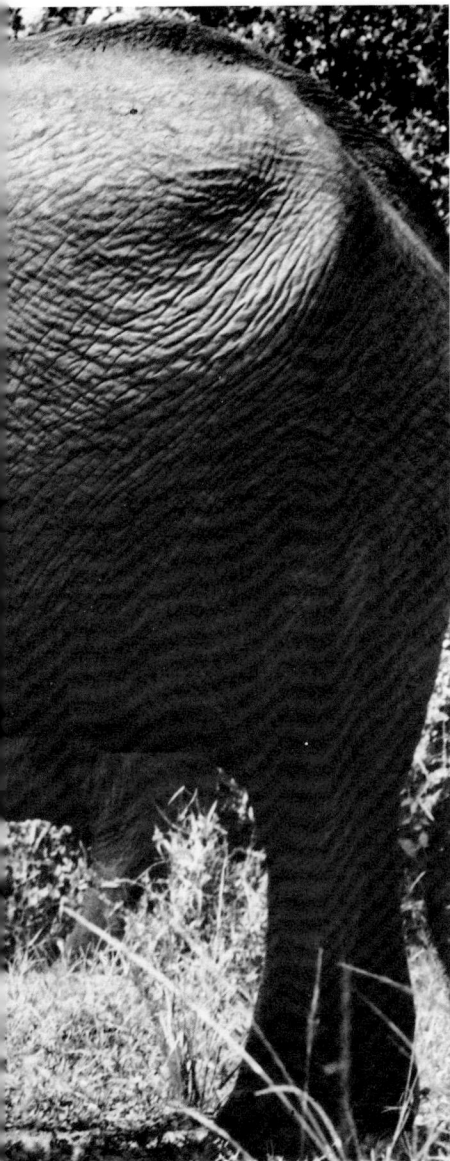

Elephants

"The longer the young animals have to grow up in a family, the further they are likely to develop. A species that is fully developed in three weeks is unlikely to reach the same level as a species that takes three years. Elephants, among the most intelligent of animals, stay together as a family for several years and the unmated females help to care for the young. Animals either started to have a family life because their young had a protracted infancy, or the new generation matured more slowly and fully because they were growing up protected by the family group."

From *Sexual Reproduction* by Susan Michelmore (The Natural History Press, Garden City, 1965).

Fox

"Cub activities do sometimes go on through the day, even though the vixen may be kenneling beneath ground only a few yards away. She is either unaware that the cubs are above ground or is not unduly concerned. Apart from mock combat—during which one cub will straddle another as they attempt to bite each other's ears and neck—digging and chewing at anything 'chewable' are the main preoccupations. Beetles are uncovered and watched with obvious interest, moths and flies are snapped at and bits of grass eaten."

From *Wild Fox* by Roger Burrows (Taplinger Publishing, New York, 1968).

Chipping Sparrows

"They hopped to the edge of the nest and remained there for some time. Then they moved gradually out into the branches of the nest tree. Sometimes one fell to the ground, and it was then led by one of the adults, usually the male, into a brushy area. By 10 days of age they could hop into the lower branches of bushes, where they sometimes remained for long periods on one perch. By 12 days of age they could fly a few feet, and at 14 days of age they were capable of sustained flight."

From "The Eastern Chipping Sparrow in Michigan" by Lawrence Harvey Walkingshaw (*Wilson Bulletin*, Vol. 56, pp. 193–205).

PHOTO CREDITS